To My Sweet Little A.J. ~ 4 yrs. old
  Happy Holydays!
         I Love you....
            Mama

Christmas
The Greatest Gift

by
Patricia Richardson Mattozzi

The Regina Press New York

Copyright © MCMXCIV Patricia Richardson Mattozzi.
All rights reserved. No part of this book may be reproduced in any
form or by any means, electronic or mechanical, including photocopying,
recording or by any information storage and retrieval system without the
written permission of the publisher.

Published by The Regina Press, Melville, NY 11747

ISBN 088271 492 9

On Christmas God sent Jesus
His gift of loving care.
Each year we celebrate His birth—
His love and joy we share.

We celebrate with happy hearts.
Candles glow so bright.

What fun to see the houses dressed in colored lights!

We sing Christmas carols
everywhere we go,

and watch from picture windows
the silent, falling snow.

Christmas is pretty bows and holly,
popcorn on a string,

candy canes and ornaments
and silver bells to ring,

packages and parties,
dresses trimmed with lace.

We share hugs and evening prayers
with cookies on a tray,
and find it hard to wait for
the dawn of Christmas Day.

Cards and letters greet us
with messages so dear,

and we send gifts and greetings
to friends both far and near.

We tell the story of Jesus
with our family on Christmas Eve,

and then in bed we dream of the gifts we might receive.

But of all the gifts at Christmas
the greatest is God's love
sent to us through Jesus.
Thank You, God, above.

*For unto you is born this day
in the city of David a Savior,
which is Christ the Lord.*

Luke 2:11